MINOR SCALE WORKBOOK

A Fun Approach to Learning Minor Scales

GLENNA BATTSON

Alfred

Note to Teachers and Parents

What is This Book?

The Minor Scale Picture Workbook is a visual approach to learning harmonic minor scale patterns. Students follow a worksheet format designed to help them discover, then remember, scale notes and fingering.

Other Features

- Explanations of half steps and whole steps.
- The patterns for natural and harmonic minor scales
- The Circle of Fifths (in two parts—Am through G♯m, then Dm through E♭m)
- Checkpoint pages (review)
- Answer pages
- Scale picture dictionary, for quick reference

Who can benefit?

- Students (especially visual learners) who are learning scales for the first time
- Students needing motivation to learn *all* the scales
- Students needing a fresh approach to reviewing scales

Why does it work?

- Students are increasingly more visual in their learning approach.
- Students respond favorably to a fun approach.
- Psychologists have proven that review is more effective when using different learning modes.

Why learn harmonic minor scales?

- Students encounter harmonic minor in many early-level pieces.
- Adjudications and auditions commonly require the harmonic minor scale.
- The sound has immediate student appeal.

Table of Contents

Understanding Half Steps and Whole Steps

HALF STEP • NO KEY BETWEEN

A half step is the distance from one key to the next, with no key between.

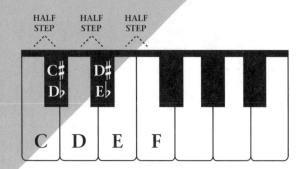

1. Draw a checkmark ✔ on the keys that are a *half step higher* than the keys marked with an X.

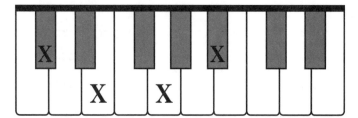

WHOLE STEP • ONE KEY BETWEEN

A whole step skips one key and is equal to two half steps.

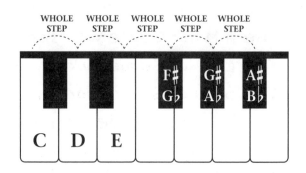

2. Draw a checkmark ✔ on the keys that are a *whole step higher* than the keys marked with an X.

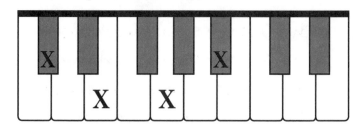

FLATS AND DOUBLE FLATS

Flats ♭ *lower* a note *one half step.*

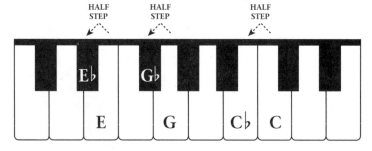

Double flats ♭♭ *lower* a note *one whole step.*

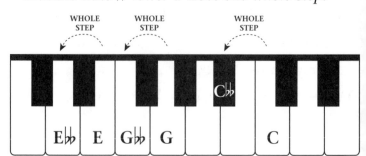

SHARPS AND DOUBLE SHARPS

Sharps ♯ *raise* a note *one half step.*

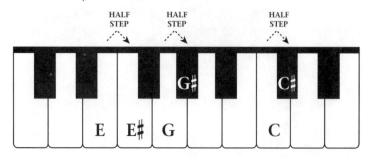

Double sharps ✕ *raise* a note *one whole step.*

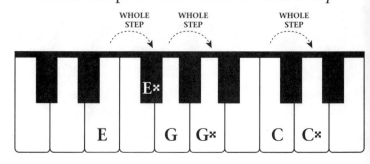

Patterns for Natural and Harmonic Minor Scales

NATURAL MINOR SCALE PATTERN

The natural minor scale is made up of eight notes, having a pattern of:

Whole step, Half step, Whole step,
Whole step, Half step, Whole step,
Whole step

(W H W • W H W • W)

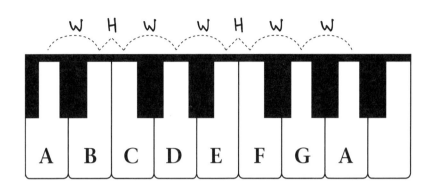

HARMONIC MINOR SCALE PATTERN

The harmonic minor scale is like the natural minor scale with the same name, except for one important change:

The 7th note is raised a half step.

The pattern becomes:

Whole step, Half step, Whole step,
Whole step, Half step, **Whole step+Half step,**
Half step

(W H W • W H **W+H** • H)

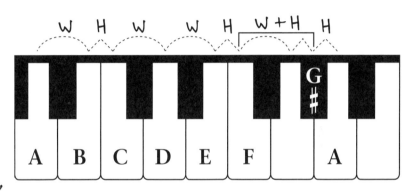

THE A HARMONIC MINOR SCALE USING TETRACHORD FINGERING (no thumbs)

1. LH finger 5 plays A.
2. LH finger 4 plays the key a whole step (W) higher.   What is it? _____
3. LH finger 3 plays the key a half step (H) higher.   What is it? _____
4. LH finger 2 plays the key a whole step (W) higher.   What is it? _____
5. RH finger 2 plays the key a whole step (W) higher.   What is it? _____
6. RH finger 3 plays the key a half step (H) higher.   What is it? _____
7. RH finger 4 plays the key a whole step plus
   a half step (W+H) higher.   What is it? _____
8. RH finger 5 plays the key a half step (H) higher.   What is it? _____

Play the A minor scale using tetrachord fingering:

```
    5   4   3   2     2   3   4   5
    └─── LH ───┘     └─── RH ───┘
```

The A Minor Scale Worksheet

STEP 1: Write the Letter Names

A. On the lines below, WRITE THE LETTERS of the music alphabet in ascending order. (The beginning and ending notes are given.)

B. To create the correct order of whole steps and half steps, use the pattern for a natural minor scale. The scale of A natural minor has no sharps or flats.

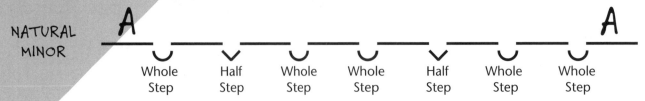

NATURAL MINOR — A _ _ _ _ _ _ A
Whole Step | Half Step | Whole Step | Whole Step | Half Step | Whole Step | Whole Step

C. To create a harmonic minor scale, copy the natural minor scale (Step 1B), then raise the 7th letter one half step by adding a SHARP (♯). *HINT: Put the ♯ to the right of the letter name.*

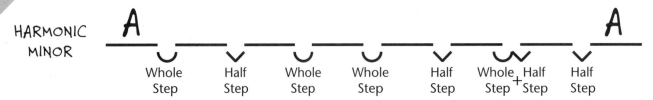

HARMONIC MINOR — A _ _ _ _ _ _ A
Whole Step | Half Step | Whole Step | Whole Step | Half Step | Whole Step + Half Step | Half Step

STEP 2: Play and Say

Using tetrachord fingering (no thumbs), play the A harmonic minor scale on the keyboard while saying the letter names. (For review, see page 5.)

STEP 3: Draw the Pattern of White and Black Keys

Use the pattern of white and black keys in the A harmonic minor scale to complete the following:

A. If the key is WHITE, circle the LOWER dot; if the key is BLACK, circle the UPPER dot.

B. Connect the circled dots.

Black Keys: ● ● ● ● ● ● ● ●

White Keys: ● ● ● ● ● ● ● ●

C. Connect the dots in the picture of **Aunty's Auto,** matching the pattern in Step 3B above.

A Minor: Aunty's Auto

STEP 4: Write the Sharp

On the grand staff below, WRITE THE SHARP needed for the A harmonic minor scale.
To create the correct order of whole steps and half steps, use the harmonic minor scale pattern.
(See Step 1C.) *HINT: Put the ♯ to the left of the note.*

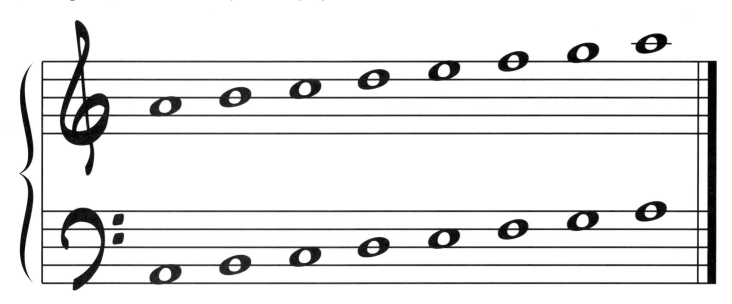

STEP 5: A Minor Key Signature

There are no sharps or flats
in the key signature of A minor.
(See Step 1B.)

*HINT: The sharp that is added to raise
the 7th letter for harmonic minor is not
included in the key signature.*

STEP 6: Play the Scale

A. Play a one-octave A harmonic minor scale while saying the note names.
Play hands separately or hands together, ascending and descending.
Use the fingering below.
*HINT: Remember the picture of **Aunty's Auto** as you play.*

RH 1 2 3 1 2 3 4 5
LH 5 4 3 2 1 3 2 1

B. Play the scale again, reading the notes of the
A harmonic minor scale (Step 4).

The E Minor Scale Worksheet

STEP 1: Write the Letter Names

A. On the lines below, WRITE THE LETTERS of the music alphabet in ascending order. (The beginning and ending notes are given.)

B. To create the correct order of whole steps and half steps, use the pattern for a natural minor scale and add a SHARP (♯) where necessary. *HINT: Put the ♯ to the right of the letter name.*

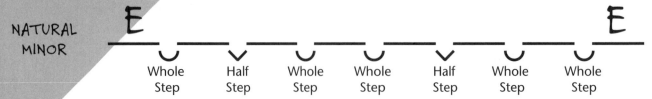

NATURAL MINOR — E ‿ Whole Step ‿ Half Step ‿ Whole Step ‿ Whole Step ‿ Half Step ‿ Whole Step ‿ Whole Step — E

C. To create a harmonic minor scale, copy the natural minor scale (Step 1B), then raise the 7th letter one half step by adding a SHARP (♯). *HINT: Put the ♯ to the right of the letter name.*

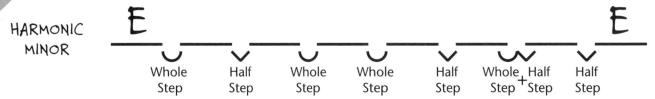

HARMONIC MINOR — E ‿ Whole Step ‿ Half Step ‿ Whole Step ‿ Whole Step ‿ Half Step ‿ Whole + Half Step ‿ Half Step — E

STEP 2: Play and Say

Using tetrachord fingering (no thumbs), play the E harmonic minor scale on the keyboard while saying the letter names. (For review, see page 5.)

STEP 3: Draw the Pattern of White and Black Keys

Use the pattern of white and black keys in the E harmonic minor scale to complete the following:

A. If the key is WHITE, circle the LOWER dot; if the key is BLACK, circle the UPPER dot.

B. Connect the circled dots.

Black Keys: ● ● ● ● ● ● ● ●

White Keys: ● ● ● ● ● ● ● ●

C. Connect the dots in the picture of the **Elf's Ears,** matching the pattern in Step 3B above.

E Minor: Elf's Ears

STEP 4: Write the Sharps

On the grand staff below, WRITE THE SHARPS needed for the E harmonic minor scale.
To create the correct order of whole steps and half steps, use the harmonic minor scale pattern.
(See Step 1C.) *HINT: Put the ♯s to the left of the notes.*

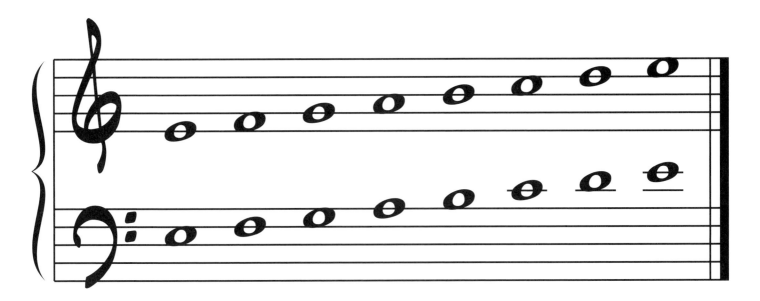

STEP 5: Circle the Key Signature

CIRCLE THE CORRECT SHARP
for the key signature of E minor.
(See Step 1B.)

*HINT: The sharp that is added to raise
the 7th letter for harmonic minor is not
included in the key signature.*

STEP 6: Play the Scale

A. Play a one-octave E harmonic minor scale while saying the note names.
Play hands separately or hands together, ascending and descending.
Use the fingering below.
*HINT: Remember the picture of the **Elf's Ears** as you play.*

RH 1 2 3 1 2 3 4 5

LH 5 4 3 2 1 3 2 1

B. Play the scale again, reading the notes of the
E harmonic minor scale (Step 4).

The B Minor Scale Worksheet

STEP 1: Write the Letter Names

A. On the lines below, WRITE THE LETTERS of the music alphabet in ascending order. (The beginning and ending notes are given.)

B. To create the correct order of whole steps and half steps, use the pattern for a natural minor scale and add SHARPS (♯s) where necessary. *HINT: Put the ♯s to the right of the letter names.*

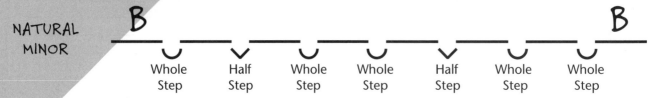

NATURAL MINOR | B _____ _____ _____ _____ _____ _____ _____ B

Whole Step — Half Step — Whole Step — Whole Step — Half Step — Whole Step — Whole Step

C. To create a harmonic minor scale, copy the natural minor scale (Step 1B), then raise the 7th letter one half step by adding a SHARP (♯). *HINT: Put the ♯ to the right of the letter name.*

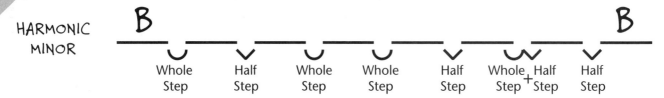

HARMONIC MINOR | B _____ _____ _____ _____ _____ _____ _____ B

Whole Step — Half Step — Whole Step — Whole Step — Half Step — Whole + Half Step — Half Step

STEP 2: Play and Say

Using tetrachord fingering (no thumbs), play the B harmonic minor scale on the keyboard while saying the letter names. (For review, see page 5.)

STEP 3: Draw the Pattern of White and Black Keys

Use the pattern of white and black keys in the B harmonic minor scale to complete the following:

A. If the key is WHITE, circle the LOWER dot; if the key is BLACK, circle the UPPER dot.

B. Connect the circled dots.

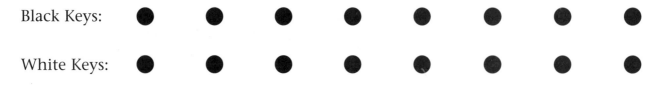

Black Keys: ● ● ● ● ● ● ● ●

White Keys: ● ● ● ● ● ● ● ●

C. Connect the dots in the picture of the **Big Buildings,** matching the pattern in Step 3B above.

B Minor: Big Buildings

STEP 4: Write the Sharps

On the grand staff below, WRITE THE SHARPS needed for the B harmonic minor scale.
To create the correct order of whole steps and half steps, use the harmonic minor scale pattern.
(See Step 1C.) *HINT: Put the ♯s to the left of the notes.*

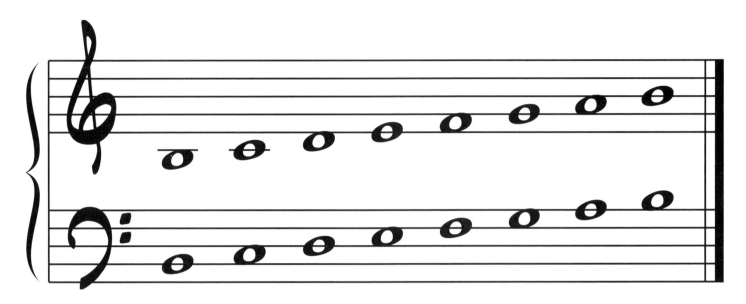

STEP 5: Circle the Key Signature

CIRCLE THE CORRECT SHARPS
for the key signature of B minor.
(See Step 1B.)

*HINT: The sharp that is added to raise
the 7th letter for harmonic minor is not
included in the key signature.*

STEP 6: Play the Scale

A. Play a one-octave B harmonic minor scale while saying the note names.
Play hands separately or hands together, ascending and descending.
Use the fingering below.
*HINT: Remember the picture of the **Big Buildings** as you play.*

RH 1 2 3 1 2 3 4 5

LH 4 3 2 1 4 3 2 1

B. Play the scale again, reading the notes lof the
B harmonic minor scale (Step 4).

The F# Minor Scale Worksheet

STEP 1: Write the Letter Names

A. On the lines below, WRITE THE LETTERS of the music alphabet in ascending order. (The beginning and ending notes are given.)

B. To create the correct order of whole steps and half steps, use the pattern for a natural minor scale and add SHARPS (♯s) where necessary. *HINT: Put the ♯s to the right of the letter names.*

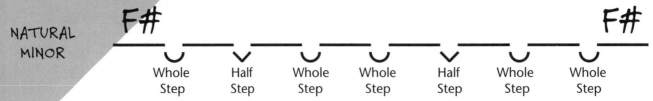

C. To create a harmonic minor scale, copy the natural minor scale (Step 1B), then raise the 7th letter one half step by adding a SHARP (♯). *HINT: Put the ♯ to the right of the letter name.*

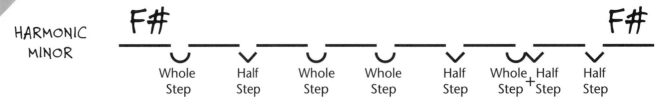

STEP 2: Play and Say

Using tetrachord fingering (no thumbs), play the F♯ harmonic minor scale on the keyboard while saying the letter names. (For review, see page 5.)

STEP 3: Draw the Pattern of White and Black Keys

Use the pattern of white and black keys in the F♯ harmonic minor scale to complete the following:

A. If the key is WHITE, circle the LOWER dot; if the key is BLACK, circle the UPPER dot.

B. Connect the circled dots.

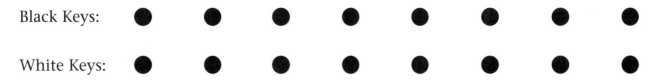

C. Connect the dots in the picture of the **Friendly Fish,** matching the pattern in Step 3B above.

F# Minor:
Friendly Fish

STEP 4: Write the Sharps

On the grand staff below, WRITE THE SHARPS needed for the F♯ harmonic minor scale.
To create the correct order of whole steps and half steps, use the harmonic minor scale pattern.
(See Step 1C.) *HINT: Put the ♯s to the left of the notes.*

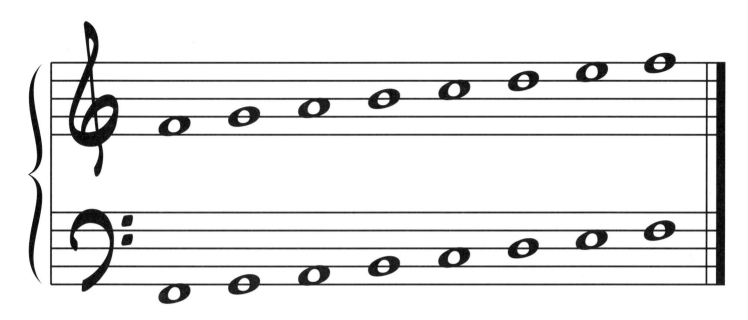

STEP 5: Circle the Key Signature

CIRCLE THE CORRECT SHARPS
for the key signature of F♯ minor.
(See Step 1B.)

*HINT: The sharp that is added to raise
the 7th letter for harmonic minor is not
included in the key signature.*

STEP 6: Play the Scale

A. Play a one-octave F♯ harmonic minor scale while saying the note names.
   Play hands separately or hands together, ascending and descending.
   Use the fingering below.
   *HINT: Remember the picture of the **Friendly Fish** as you play.*

   RH 3 4 1 2 3 1 2 3
   LH 4 3 2 1 3 2 1 4

B. Play the scale again, reading the notes of the
   F♯ harmonic minor scale (Step 4).

The C# Minor Scale Worksheet

STEP 1: **Write the Letter Names**

A. On the lines below, WRITE THE LETTERS of the music alphabet in ascending order. (The beginning and ending notes are given.)

B. To create the correct order of whole steps and half steps, use the pattern for a natural minor scale and add SHARPS (♯s) where necessary. *HINT: Put the ♯s to the right of the letter names.*

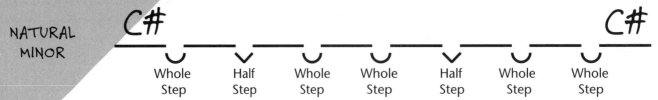

C. To create a harmonic minor scale, copy the natural minor scale (Step 1B), then raise the 7th letter one half step by adding a SHARP (♯). *HINT: Put the ♯ to the right of the letter name.*

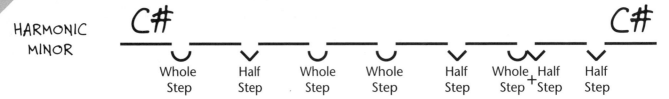

STEP 2: **Play and Say**

Using tetrachord fingering (no thumbs), play the C♯ harmonic minor scale on the keyboard while saying the letter names. (For review, see page 5.)

STEP 3: **Draw the Pattern of White and Black Keys**

Use the pattern of white and black keys in the C♯ harmonic minor scale to complete the following:

A. If the key is WHITE, circle the LOWER dot; if the key is BLACK, circle the UPPER dot.

B. Connect the circled dots.

Black Keys: ● ● ● ● ● ● ● ●

White Keys: ● ● ● ● ● ● ● ●

C. Connect the dots in the picture of the **Crying Clown,** matching the pattern in Step 3B above.

C# Minor:
Crying Clown

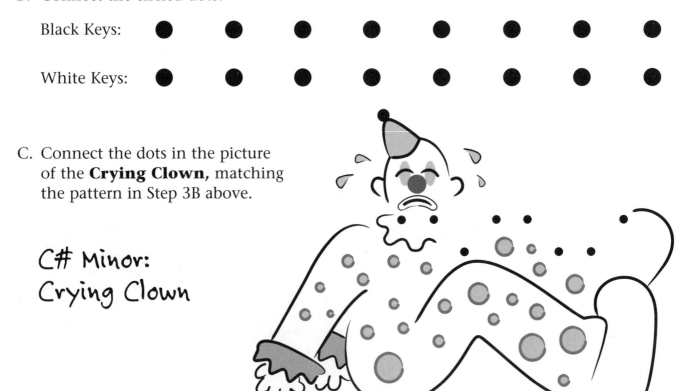

STEP 4: Write the Sharps

On the grand staff below, WRITE THE SHARPS needed for the C# harmonic minor scale.
To create the correct order of whole steps and half steps, use the harmonic minor scale pattern.
(See Step 1C.) *HINT: Put the #s to the left of the notes.*

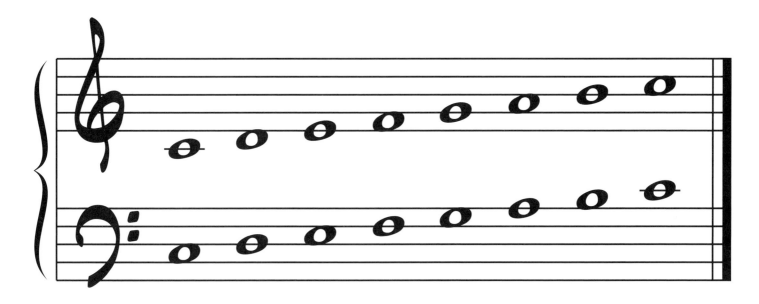

STEP 5: Circle the Key Signature

CIRCLE THE CORRECT SHARPS
for the key signature of C# minor.
(See Step 1B.)

*HINT: The sharp that is added to raise
the 7th letter for harmonic minor is not
included in the key signature.*

STEP 6: Play the Scale

A. Play a one-octave C# harmonic minor scale while saying the note names.
Play hands separately or hands together, ascending and descending.
Use the fingering below.
*HINT: Remember the picture of the **Crying Clown** as you play.*

RH 3 4 1 2 3 1 2 3

LH 3 2 1 4 3 2 1 3

B. Play the scale again, reading the notes of the
C# harmonic minor scale (Step 4).

The G# Minor Scale Worksheet

STEP 1: Write the Letter Names

A. On the lines below, WRITE THE LETTERS of the music alphabet in ascending order.
(The beginning and ending notes are given.)

B. To create the correct order of whole steps and half steps, use the pattern for a natural minor scale and add SHARPS (♯s) where necessary. *HINT: Put the ♯s to the right of the letter names.*

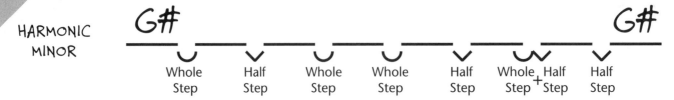

NATURAL MINOR

G#   G#

Whole Step   Half Step   Whole Step   Whole Step   Half Step   Whole Step   Whole Step

C. To create a harmonic minor scale, copy the natural minor scale (Step 1B), then raise the 7th letter one half step by adding a DOUBLE SHARP (𝄪). *HINT: Put the 𝄪 to the right of the letter name.*

HARMONIC MINOR

G#   G#

Whole Step   Half Step   Whole Step   Whole Step   Half Step   Whole Step + Half Step   Half Step

STEP 2: Play and Say

Using tetrachord fingering (no thumbs), play the G♯ harmonic minor scale on the keyboard while saying the letter names. (For review, see page 5.)

STEP 3: Draw the Pattern of White and Black Keys

Use the pattern of white and black keys in the G♯ harmonic minor scale to complete the following:

A. If the key is WHITE, circle the LOWER dot; if the key is BLACK, circle the UPPER dot.

B. Connect the circled dots.

Black Keys: ●   ●   ●   ●   ●   ●   ●   ●

White Keys: ●   ●   ●   ●   ●   ●   ●   ●

C. Connect the dots in the picture of **Grandpa's Goatee,** matching the pattern in Step 3B above.

G# Minor:
Grandpa's Goatee

STEP 4: Write the Sharps and Double Sharp

On the grand staff below, WRITE THE SHARPS AND THE DOUBLE SHARP needed for the G♯ harmonic minor scale. To create the correct order of whole steps and half steps, use the harmonic minor scale pattern. (See Step 1C.) *HINT: Put the ♯s and the 𝄪 to the left of the notes.*

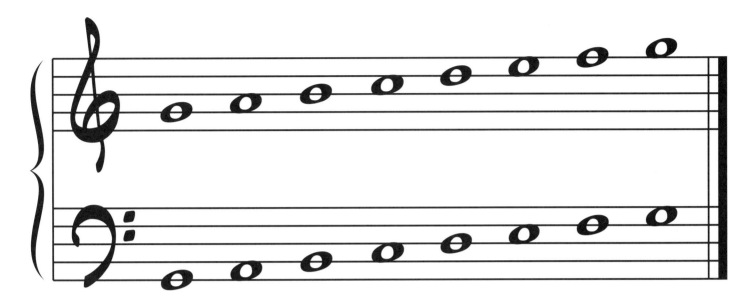

STEP 5: Circle the Key Signature

CIRCLE THE CORRECT SHARPS for the key signature of G♯ minor. (See Step 1B.)

HINT: The double sharp that is added to raise the 7th letter for harmonic minor does not change the key signature.

STEP 6: Play the Scale

A. Play a one-octave G♯ harmonic minor scale while saying the note names. Play hands separately or hands together, ascending and descending. Use the fingering below.
*HINT: Remember the picture of **Grandpa's Goatee** as you play.*

RH 3 4 1 2 3 1 2 3

LH 3 2 1 4 3 2 1 3

B. Play the scale again, reading the notes of the G♯ harmonic minor scale (Step 4).

18

The Circle of Fifths

The Circle of Fifths is a handy tool to help you see how scales are related to each other. Moving clockwise, the order is Am, Em, Bm, F#m, C#m, G#m. Scales are often played in this order. (You will learn the rest of the Circle of Fifths on page 32.)

Fill in the blanks with the *names* of the sharps in the key signature of each scale. *Remember:* The *natural* minor scale tells the key signature. (See Scale Worksheets Step 1B.)

Em ___
Bm ___ ___
F#m ___ ___ ___
C#m ___ ___ ___ ___
G#m ___ ___ ___ ___ ___

Circle diagram labels: Am — no #s no bs; Em — 1#; Bm — 2 #s; F#m — 3 #s; C#m — 4 #s; G#m — 5 #s

Moving Around the Circle of Fifths

To remember the order of the sharp scales, start at the *top* of the circle and move clockwise.

1. Play the A harmonic minor scale. Stop on the 5th tone. **The 5th tone is ___.**
   This is the first note of the next scale around the Circle of Fifths.

2. Play the E harmonic minor scale. Stop on the 5th tone. **The 5th tone is ___.**
   This is the first note of the next scale around the Circle of Fifths.

3. Play the B harmonic minor scale. Stop on the 5th tone. **The 5th tone is ___.**
   This is the first note of the next scale around the Circle of Fifths.

4. Play the F♯ harmonic minor scale. Stop on the 5th tone. **The 5th tone is ___.**
   This is the first note of the next scale around the Circle of Fifths.

5. Play the C♯ harmonic minor scale. Stop on the 5th tone. **The 5th tone is ___.**
   This is the first note of the next scale around the Circle of Fifths.

Answers Em: F♯ Bm: F♯ C♯ F♯m: F♯ C♯ G♯ C♯m: F♯ C♯ G♯ D♯ G♯m: F♯ C♯ G♯ D♯ A♯

1. E 2. B 3. F♯ 4. C♯ 5. G♯

Minor Scale Checkpoint No. 1

Color the star or cover it with a sticker of your choice, when you play the following without mistakes. Ask your teacher whether you should play hands separately or hands together.

Remember the pictures as you play!

    1. In *Circle of Fifths* order, play the harmonic minor scales you have learned:
Am Em Bm F♯m C♯m G♯m

    2. In *alphabetical* order, play the harmonic minor scales you have learned:
Am Bm C♯m Em F♯m G♯m
(You have not learned Dm yet.)

Fill in the blanks below. Each correct answer counts as 1 point.

1. A half step is the distance from one key to the next, with _____ key between.

2. A whole step is equal to two half steps. Skip _____ key for a whole step.

3. The pattern for a natural minor scale is W H W W H _____ _____.

4. The pattern for a harmonic minor scale is W H W W H _____ _____.

5. There are _____ flats or sharps in the key signature of A minor.

6. There are 4 _____ in the key signature of C♯ minor.

7. In the B minor scale, the LH begins with finger _____.

8. In the E minor scale, RH finger 1 plays E and _____.

9. In the G♯ minor scale, LH finger 1 plays _____ and _____.

10.    This is the picture for the scale of _____ harmonic minor.
Its name is the _____ _____.

Your score: _____
(Perfect score = 10)

The D Minor Scale Worksheet

STEP 1: Write the Letter Names

A. On the lines below, WRITE THE LETTERS of the music alphabet in ascending order. (The beginning and ending notes are given.)

B. To create the correct order of whole steps and half steps, use the pattern for a natural minor scale and add a FLAT (♭) where necessary. *HINT: Put the ♭ to the right of the letter name.*

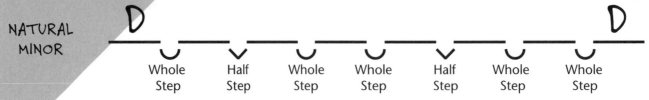

NATURAL MINOR

D   D

Whole Step | Half Step | Whole Step | Whole Step | Half Step | Whole Step | Whole Step

C. To create a harmonic minor scale, copy the natural minor scale (Step 1B), then raise the 7th letter one half step by adding a SHARP (♯). *HINT: Put the ♯ to the right of the letter name.*

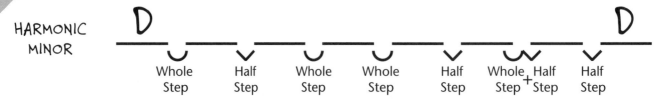

HARMONIC MINOR

D   D

Whole Step | Half Step | Whole Step | Whole Step | Half Step | Whole Step + Half Step | Half Step

STEP 2: Play and Say

Using tetrachord fingering (no thumbs), play the D harmonic minor scale on the keyboard while saying the letter names. (For review, see page 5.)

STEP 3: Draw the Pattern of White and Black Keys

Use the pattern of white and black keys in the D harmonic minor scale to complete the following:

A. If the key is WHITE, circle the LOWER dot; if the key is BLACK, circle the UPPER dot.

B. Connect the circled dots.

Black Keys: ● ● ● ● ● ● ● ●

White Keys: ● ● ● ● ● ● ● ●

C. Connect the dots in the picture of the **Diesel Delivery,** matching the pattern in Step 3B above.

D Minor: Diesel Delivery

STEP 4: Write the Flat and Sharp

On the grand staff below, WRITE THE FLAT and SHARP needed for the D harmonic minor scale. To create the correct order of whole steps and half steps, use the harmonic minor scale pattern. (See Step 1C.) HINT: *Put the ♭ and ♯ to the left of the notes.*

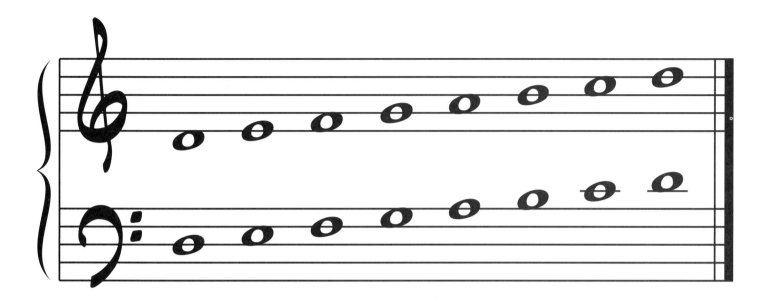

STEP 5: Circle the Key Signature

CIRCLE THE CORRECT FLAT for the key signature of D minor. (See Step 1B.)

HINT: The sharp that is added to raise the 7th letter for harmonic minor is not included in the key signature.

STEP 6: Play the Scale

A. Play a one-octave D harmonic minor scale while saying the note names. Play hands separately or hands together, ascending and descending. Use the fingering below.
*HINT: Remember the picture of the **Diesel Delivery** as you play.*

RH 1 2 3 1 2 3 4 5

LH 5 4 3 2 1 3 2 1

B. Play the scale again, reading the notes of the D harmonic minor scale (Step 4).

The G Minor Scale Worksheet

STEP 1: Write the Letter Names

A. On the lines below, WRITE THE LETTERS of the music alphabet in ascending order. (The beginning and ending notes are given.)

B. To create the correct order of whole steps and half steps, use the pattern for a natural minor scale and add FLATS (♭s) where necessary. *HINT: Put the ♭s to the right of the letter names.*

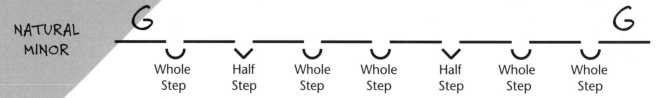

NATURAL MINOR

G   G

Whole Step   Half Step   Whole Step   Whole Step   Half Step   Whole Step   Whole Step

C. To create a harmonic minor scale, copy the natural minor scale (Step 1B), then raise the 7th letter one half step by adding a SHARP (♯). *HINT: Put the ♯ to the right of the letter name.*

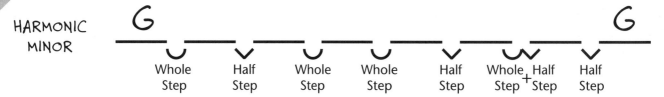

HARMONIC MINOR

G   G

Whole Step   Half Step   Whole Step   Whole Step   Half Step   Whole+Half Step   Half Step

STEP 2: Play and Say

Using tetrachord fingering (no thumbs), play the G harmonic minor scale on the keyboard while saying the letter names. (For review, see page 5.)

STEP 3: Draw the Pattern of White and Black Keys

Use the pattern of white and black keys in the G harmonic minor scale to complete the following:

A. If the key is WHITE, circle the LOWER dot; if the key is BLACK, circle the UPPER dot.

B. Connect the circled dots.

Black Keys: ●   ●   ●   ●   ●   ●   ●   ●

White Keys: ●   ●   ●   ●   ●   ●   ●   ●

C. Connect the dots in the picture of the **Giant Greeting,** matching the pattern in Step 3B above.

G Minor: Giant Greeting

STEP 4: Write the Flats and Sharp

On the grand staff below, WRITE THE FLATS and SHARP needed for the G harmonic minor scale.
To create the correct order of whole steps and half steps, use the harmonic minor scale pattern.
(See Step 1C.) *HINT: Put the ♭s and ♯ to the left of the notes.*

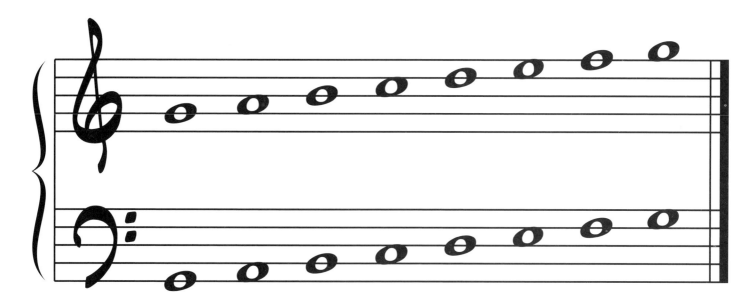

STEP 5: Circle the Key Signature

CIRCLE THE CORRECT FLATS
for the key signature of G minor.
(See Step 1B.)

*HINT: The sharp that is added to raise
the 7th letter for harmonic minor is not
included in the key signature.*

STEP 6: Play the Scale

A. Play a one-octave G harmonic minor scale while saying the note names.
Play hands separately or hands together, ascending and descending.
Use the fingering below.
*HINT: Remember the picture of the **Giant Greeting** as you play.*

RH 1 2 3 1 2 3 4 5

LH 5 4 3 2 1 3 2 1

B. Play the scale again, reading the notes of the
G harmonic minor scale (Step 4).

The C Minor Scale Worksheet

STEP 1: Write the Letter Names

A. On the lines below, WRITE THE LETTERS of the music alphabet in ascending order.
(The beginning and ending notes are given.)

B. To create the correct order of whole steps and half steps, use the pattern for a natural minor
scale and add FLATS (♭s) where necessary. *HINT: Put the ♭s to the right of the letter names.*

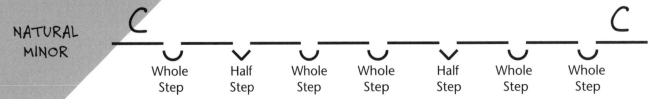

NATURAL MINOR — C _____ _____ _____ _____ _____ _____ C

| Whole Step | Half Step | Whole Step | Whole Step | Half Step | Whole Step | Whole Step |

C. To create a harmonic minor scale, copy the natural minor scale (Step 1B), then raise the 7th letter
one half step by replacing the flat with a NATURAL (♮). *HINT: Put the ♮ to the right of the letter nam*

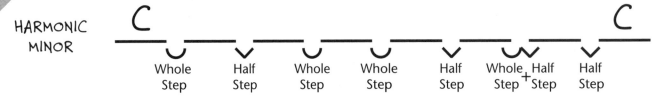

HARMONIC MINOR — C _____ _____ _____ _____ _____ _____ C

| Whole Step | Half Step | Whole Step | Whole Step | Half Step | Whole + Half Step | Half Step |

STEP 2: Play and Say

Using tetrachord fingering (no thumbs), play the C harmonic minor scale on the keyboard
while saying the letter names. (For review, see page 5.)

STEP 3: Draw the Pattern of White and Black Keys

Use the pattern of white and black keys in the C harmonic minor scale to complete the following:

A. If the key is WHITE, circle the LOWER dot; if the key is BLACK, circle the UPPER dot.

B. Connect the circled dots.

Black Keys: ●   ●   ●   ●   ●   ●   ●   ●

White Keys: ●   ●   ●   ●   ●   ●   ●   ●

C. Connect the dots in the picture
of the **Crystal Crown,** matching
the pattern in Step 3B above.

C Minor: Crystal Crown

STEP 4: Write the Flats and Natural

On the grand staff below, WRITE THE FLATS and NATURAL needed for the C harmonic minor scale. To create the correct order of whole steps and half steps, use the harmonic minor scale pattern. (See Step 1C.) *HINT: Put the ♭s and ♮ to the left of the notes.*

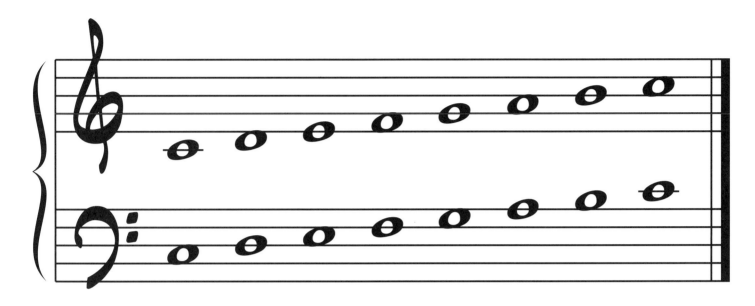

STEP 5: Circle the Key Signature

CIRCLE THE CORRECT FLATS for the key signature of C minor. (See Step 1B.)

HINT: The natural that replaces the flat for the 7th letter in harmonic minor does not change the key signature.

STEP 6: Play the Scale

A. Play a one-octave C harmonic minor scale while saying the note names. Play hands separately or hands together, ascending and descending. Use the fingering below.
*HINT: Remember the picture of the **Crystal Crown** as you play.*

RH 1 2 3 1 2 3 4 5

LH 5 4 3 2 1 3 2 1

B. Play the scale again, reading the notes of the C harmonic minor scale (Step 4).

The F Minor Scale Worksheet

STEP 1: Write the Letter Names

A. On the lines below, WRITE THE LETTERS of the music alphabet in ascending order. (The beginning and ending notes are given.)

B. To create the correct order of whole steps and half steps, use the pattern for a natural minor scale and add FLATS (♭s) where necessary. *HINT: Put the ♭s to the right of the letter names.*

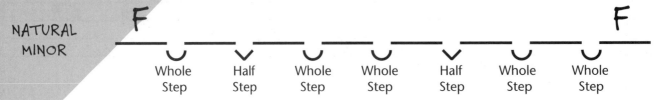

C. To create a harmonic minor scale, copy the natural minor scale (Step 1B), then raise the 7th letter one half step by replacing the flat with a NATURAL (♮). *HINT: Put the ♮ to the right of the letter nar...*

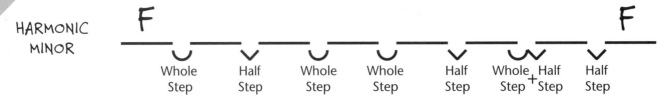

STEP 2: Play and Say

Using tetrachord fingering (no thumbs), play the F harmonic minor scale on the keyboard while saying the letter names. (For review, see page 5.)

STEP 3: Draw the Pattern of White and Black Keys

Use the pattern of white and black keys in the F harmonic minor scale to complete the following:

A. If the key is WHITE, circle the LOWER dot; if the key is BLACK, circle the UPPER dot.

B. Connect the circled dots.

C. Connect the dots in the picture of **Fred's Farm,** matching the pattern in Step 3B above.

F Minor: Fred's Farm

STEP 4: Write the Flats and Natural

On the grand staff below, WRITE THE FLATS and NATURAL needed for the F harmonic minor scale. To create the correct order of whole steps and half steps, use the harmonic minor scale pattern. (See Step 1C.) *HINT: Put the ♭s and ♮ to the left of the notes.*

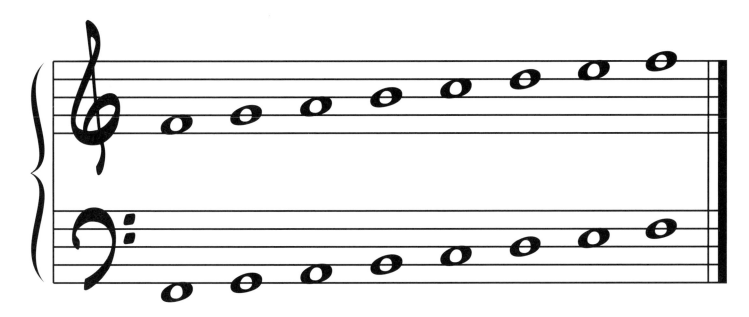

STEP 5: Circle the Key Signature

CIRCLE THE CORRECT FLATS
for the key signature of F minor.
(See Step 1B.)

*HINT: The natural that replaces the flat
for the 7th letter in harmonic minor does
not change the key signature.*

STEP 6: Play the Scale

A. Play a one-octave F harmonic minor scale while saying the note names.
   Play hands separately or hands together, ascending and descending.
   Use the fingering below.
   *HINT: Remember the picture of **Fred's Farm** as you play.*

RH 1 2 3 4 1 2 3 4

LH 5 4 3 2 1 3 2 1

B. Play the scale again, reading the notes of the
   F harmonic minor scale (Step 4).

The Bb Minor Scale Worksheet

STEP 1: Write the Letter Names

A. On the lines below, WRITE THE LETTERS of the music alphabet in ascending order. (The beginning and ending notes are given.)

B. To create the correct order of whole steps and half steps, use the pattern for a natural minor scale and add FLATS (♭s) where necessary. *HINT: Put the ♭s to the right of the letter names.*

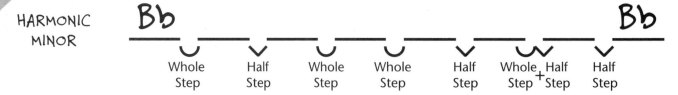

NATURAL MINOR — Bb _____ _____ _____ _____ _____ _____ Bb

Whole Step · Half Step · Whole Step · Whole Step · Half Step · Whole Step · Whole Step

C. To create a harmonic minor scale, copy the natural minor scale (Step 1B), then raise the 7th letter one half step by replacing the flat with a NATURAL (♮). *HINT: Put the ♮ to the right of the letter nam...*

HARMONIC MINOR — Bb _____ _____ _____ _____ _____ _____ Bb

Whole Step · Half Step · Whole Step · Whole Step · Half Step · Whole Step + Half Step · Half Step

STEP 2: Play and Say

Using tetrachord fingering (no thumbs), play the B♭ harmonic minor scale on the keyboard while saying the letter names. (For review, see page 5.)

STEP 3: Draw the Pattern of White and Black Keys

Use the pattern of white and black keys in the B♭ harmonic minor scale to complete the following:

A. If the key is WHITE, circle the LOWER dot; if the key is BLACK, circle the UPPER dot.

B. Connect the circled dots.

Black Keys: ● ● ● ● ● ● ● ●

White Keys: ● ● ● ● ● ● ● ●

C. Connect the dots in the picture of the **Baby's Buggy,** matching the pattern in Step 3B above.

Bb Minor: Baby's Buggy

STEP 4: Write the Flats and Natural

On the grand staff below, WRITE THE FLATS and NATURAL needed for the B♭ harmonic minor scale. To create the correct order of whole steps and half steps, use the harmonic minor scale pattern. (See Step 1C.) *HINT: Put the ♭s and ♮ to the left of the notes.*

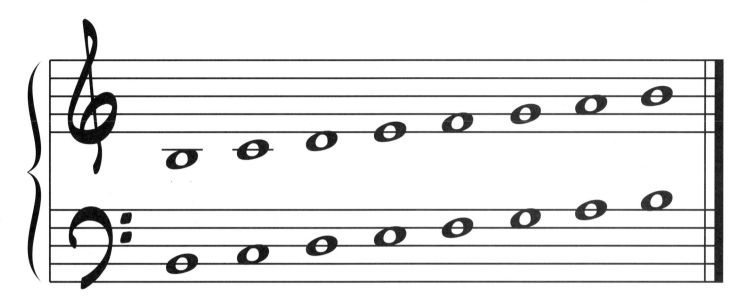

STEP 5: Circle the Key Signature

CIRCLE THE CORRECT FLATS for the key signature of B♭ minor. (See Step 1B.)

HINT: The natural that replaces the flat for the 7th letter in harmonic minor does not change the key signature.

STEP 6: Play the Scale

A. Play a one-octave B♭ harmonic minor scale while saying the note names. Play hands separately or hands together, ascending and descending. Use the fingering below.
*HINT: Remember the picture of the **Baby's Buggy** as you play.*

RH 4 1 2 3 1 2 3 4
LH 2 1 3 2 1 4 3 2

B. Play the scale again, reading the notes of the B♭ harmonic minor scale (Step 4).

The Eb Minor Scale Worksheet

STEP 1: Write the Letter Names

A. On the lines below, WRITE THE LETTERS of the music alphabet in ascending order.
(The beginning and ending notes are given.)

B. To create the correct order of whole steps and half steps, use the pattern for a natural minor
scale and add FLATS (♭s) where necessary. *HINT: Put the ♭s to the right of the letter names.*

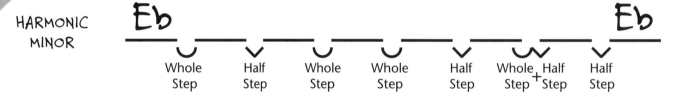

NATURAL
MINOR

Eb _____ Eb

Whole Step   Half Step   Whole Step   Whole Step   Half Step   Whole Step   Whole Step

C. To create a harmonic minor scale, copy the natural minor scale (Step 1B), then raise the 7th letter
one half step by replacing the flat with a NATURAL (♮). *HINT: Put the ♮ to the right of the letter nam*

HARMONIC
MINOR

Eb _____ Eb

Whole Step   Half Step   Whole Step   Whole Step   Half Step   Whole Step + Half Step   Half Step

STEP 2: Play and Say

Using tetrachord fingering (no thumbs), play the Eb harmonic minor scale on the keyboard
while saying the letter names. (For review, see page 5.)

STEP 3: Draw the Pattern of White and Black Keys

Use the pattern of white and black keys in the Eb harmonic minor scale to complete the following:

A. If the key is WHITE, circle the LOWER dot; if the key is BLACK, circle the UPPER dot.

B. Connect the circled dots.

Black Keys: ●   ●   ●   ●   ●   ●   ●   ●

White Keys: ●   ●   ●   ●   ●   ●   ●   ●

C. Connect the dots in the picture of
the **Elephant's Ego,** matching
the pattern in Step 3B above.

Eb Minor:
Elephant's Ego

STEP 4: Write the Flats and Natural

On the grand staff below, WRITE THE FLATS and NATURAL needed for the E♭ harmonic minor scale. To create the correct order of whole steps and half steps, use the harmonic minor scale pattern. (See Step 1C.) *HINT: Put the ♭s and ♮ to the left of the notes.*

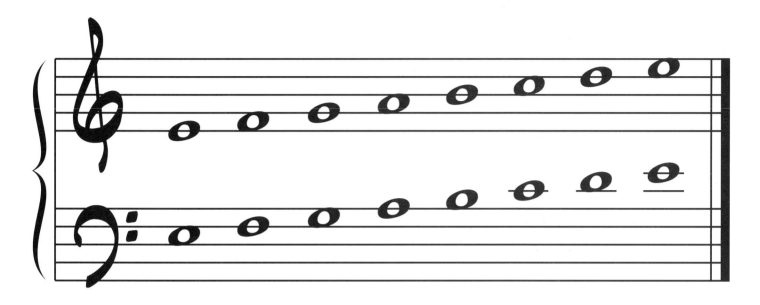

STEP 5: Circle the Key Signature

CIRCLE THE CORRECT FLATS for the key signature of E♭ minor. (See Step 1B.)

HINT: The natural that replaces the flat for the 7th letter in harmonic minor does not change the key signature.

STEP 6: Play the Scale

A. Play a one-octave E♭ harmonic minor scale while saying the note names. Play hands separately or hands together, ascending and descending. Use the fingering below.
   *HINT: Remember the picture of the **Elephant's Ego** as you play.*

RH 3 1 2 3 4 1 2 3

LH 2 1 4 3 2 1 3 2

B. Play the scale again, reading the notes of the E♭ harmonic minor scale (Step 4).

Continuing the Circle of Fifths

On page 18 you learned the first half of the Circle of Fifths, from Am clockwise through G#m. Continuing clockwise, the order is Ebm, Bbm, Fm, Cm, Gm, Dm. Scales are often played in this order.

Fill in the blanks with the *names* of the flats in the key signature of each scale. *Remember:* The *natural* minor scale tells the key signature. (See Scale Worksheets Step 1B.)

Ebm __ __ __

         __ __ __

Bbm __ __ __ __ __

Fm   __ __ __ __

Cm   __ __ __

Gm   __ __

Dm   __

Moving Around the Circle of Fifths

To remember the order of the flat scales, start at the *bottom* of the circle and move clockwise.

1. Play the Eb harmonic minor scale. Stop on the 5th tone. **The 5th tone is ____.**
   This is the first note of the next scale around the Circle of Fifths.

2. Play the Bb harmonic minor scale. Stop on the 5th tone. **The 5th tone is ____.**
   This is the first note of the next scale around the Circle of Fifths.

3. Play the F harmonic minor scale. Stop on the 5th tone. **The 5th tone is ____.**
   This is the first note of the next scale around the Circle of Fifths.

4. Play the C harmonic minor scale. Stop on the 5th tone. **The 5th tone is ____.**
   This is the first note of the next scale around the Circle of Fifths.

5. Play the G harmonic minor scale. Stop on the 5th tone. **The 5th tone is ____.**
   This is the first note of the next scale around the Circle of Fifths.

Minor Scale Checkpoint No. 2

Color the star or cover it with a sticker of your choice, when you play the following
without mistakes. Ask your teacher whether you should play hands separately
or hands together.

Remember the pictures as you play!

 1. In *Circle of Fifths* order, play the new harmonic minor scales you have learned:
E♭m B♭m Fm Cm Gm Dm

 2. In *Circle of Fifths* order, play *all* the harmonic minor scales:
Am Em Bm F♯m C♯m G♯m E♭m B♭m Fm Cm Gm Dm

 3. In *alphabetical* order, play *all* the harmonic minor scales:
Am B♭m Bm Cm C♯m Dm E♭m Em Fm F♯m Gm G♯m

Fill in the blanks below. Each correct answer counts as 1 point.

1. There are _____ flats in the key signature of E♭ minor.

2. There are 5 _____ in the key signature of B♭ minor.

3. When playing the F harmonic minor scale, RH finger 1 plays _____ and _____.

4. This is the picture for the scale of _____ harmonic minor.

   Its name is the _____ _____.

5. When playing the E♭ harmonic minor scale, LH finger 1 plays _____ and _____.

6. The name of the raised 7th in G harmonic minor is _____.

7. The name of the raised 7th in D harmonic minor is _____.

8. The names of the two black keys in the scale of C harmonic minor
   are _____ and _____.

Your score: _____
(Perfect score = 8)

Answers 1. 6 2. flats 3. F, C 4. D, Diesel Delivery 5. E, C♭ 6. F♯ 7. C♯ 8. E♭, A♭

Worksheet Answers: STEP 1

A minor, page 6:	A	B	C	D	E	F	G	A
E minor, page 8:	E	F#	G	A	B	C	D	E
B minor, page 10:	B	C#	D	E	F#	G	A	B
F# minor, page 12:	F#	G#	A	B	C#	D	E	F#
C# minor, page 14:	C#	D#	E	F#	G#	A	B	C#
G# minor, page 16:	G#	A#	B	C#	D#	E	F#	G#
D minor, page 20:	D	E	F	G	A	Bb	C	D
G minor, page 22:	G	A	Bb	C	D	Eb	F	G
C minor, page 24:	C	D	Eb	F	G	Ab	Bb	C
F minor, page 26:	F	G	Ab	Bb	C	Db	Eb	F
Bb minor, page 28:	Bb	C	Db	Eb	F	Gb	Ab	Bb
Eb minor, page 30:	Eb	F	Gb	Ab	Bb	Cb	Db	Eb

Worksheet Answers: STEP 2

A minor, page 6:	A	B	C	D	E	F	G#	A
E minor, page 8:	E	F#	G	A	B	C	D#	E
B minor, page 10:	B	C#	D	E	F#	G	A#	B
F# minor, page 12:	F#	G#	A	B	C#	D	E#	F#
C# minor, page 14:	C#	D#	E	F#	G#	A	B#	C#
G# minor, page 16:	G#	A#	B	C#	D#	E	F✕	G#
D minor, page 20:	D	E	F	G	A	Bb	C#	D
G minor, page 22:	G	A	Bb	C	D	Eb	F#	G
C minor, page 24:	C	D	Eb	F	G	Ab	B♮	C
F minor, page 26:	F	G	Ab	Bb	C	Db	E♮	F
Bb minor, page 28:	Bb	C	Db	Eb	F	Gb	A♮	Bb
Eb minor, page 30:	Eb	F	Gb	Ab	Bb	Cb	D♮	Eb

Worksheet Answers: STEP 3

A harmonic minor, page 6:

E harmonic minor, page 8:

B harmonic minor, page 10:

F# harmonic minor, page 12:

C# harmonic minor, page 14:

G# harmonic minor, page 16:

D harmonic minor, page 20:

G harmonic minor, page 22:

C harmonic minor, page 24:

F harmonic minor, page 26:

Bb harmonic minor, page 28:

Eb harmonic minor, page 30:

Worksheet Answers: STEP 4

A harmonic minor, page 7

E harmonic minor, page 9

B harmonic minor, page 11

F# harmonic minor, page 13

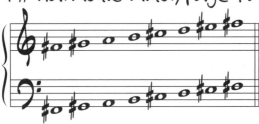

C# harmonic minor, page 15

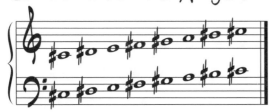

G# harmonic minor, page 17

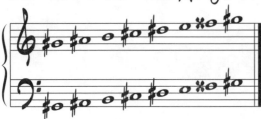

D harmonic minor, page 21

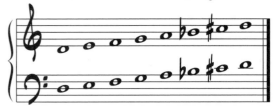

G harmonic minor, page 23

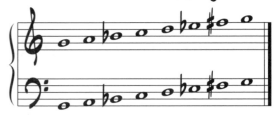

C harmonic minor, page 25

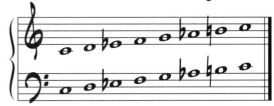

F harmonic minor, page 27

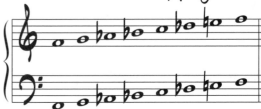

Bb harmonic minor, page 29

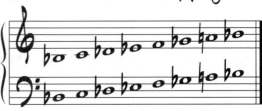

Eb harmonic minor, page 31

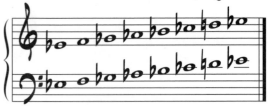

Worksheet Answers: STEP 5

A minor,
page 7:

D minor,
page 21:

E minor,
page 9:

G minor,
page 23:

B minor,
page 11:

C minor,
page 25:

F# minor,
page 13:

F minor,
page 27:

C# minor,
page 15:

Bb minor,
page 29:

G# minor,
page 17:

Eb minor,
page 31:

Enharmonic Scales

Enharmonic scales sound alike and are played alike, but they are spelled differently and have different key signatures. (The pictures are also the same. They just have different names.) Use the letter names of the natural minor scale to find how many flats or sharps are in the key signature. (Remember that the first and last notes are the same.)

G# Minor: Grandpa's Goatee

Natural Minor: G# A# B C# D# E F# G#
G# minor has ____ sharps.

Harmonic Minor: G# A# B C# D# E F𝄪 G#

Ab Minor: Agreeable Archaeologist

Natural Minor: Ab Bb Cb Db Eb Fb Gb Ab
Ab minor has ____ flats.

Harmonic Minor: Ab Bb Cb Db Eb Fb G♮ Ab

Bb Minor: Baby's Buggy

Natural Minor: Bb C Db Eb F Gb Ab Bb
Bb minor has ____ flats.

Harmonic Minor: Bb C Db Eb F Gb A♮ Bb

A# Minor: Adoring Aunty

Natural Minor: A# B# C# D# E# F# G# A#
A# minor has ____ sharps.

Harmonic Minor: A# B# C# D# E# F# G𝄪 A#

Eb Minor: Elephant's Ego

Natural Minor: Eb F Gb Ab Bb Cb Db Eb
Eb minor has ____ flats.

Harmonic Minor: Eb F Gb Ab Bb Cb D♮ Eb

D# Minor: Daring Dreamer

Natural Minor: D# E# F# G# A# B C# D#
D# minor has ____ sharps.

Harmonic Minor: D# E# F# G# A# B C𝄪 D#

Answers G#m: 5 Abm: 7 Bbm: 5 A#m: 7 Ebm: 6 D#m: 6

Minor Scale Picture Dictionary

A Minor: Aunty's Auto

RH 1 2 3 1 2 3 4 5
LH 5 4 3 2 1 3 2 1

E Minor: Elf's Ears

RH 1 2 3 1 2 3 4 5
LH 5 4 3 2 1 3 2 1

B Minor: Big Buildings

RH 1 2 3 1 2 3 4 5
LH 4 3 2 1 4 3 2 1

F# Minor: Friendly Fish

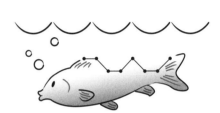

RH 3 4 1 2 3 1 2 3
LH 4 3 2 1 3 2 1 4

C# Minor: Crying Clown

RH 3 4 1 2 3 1 2 3
LH 3 2 1 4 3 2 1 3

G# Minor: Grandpa's Goatee

RH 3 4 1 2 3 1 2 3
LH 3 2 1 4 3 2 1 3

Ab Minor: Agreeable Archaeologist

RH 3 4 1 2 3 1 2 3
LH 3 2 1 4 3 2 1 3

Minor Scale Picture Dictionary

D Minor: Diesel Delivery

RH 1 2 3 1 2 3 4 5
LH 5 4 3 2 1 3 2 1

G Minor: Giant Greeting

RH 1 2 3 1 2 3 4 5
LH 5 4 3 2 1 3 2 1

C Minor: Crystal Crown

RH 1 2 3 1 2 3 4 5
LH 5 4 3 2 1 3 2 1

F Minor: Fred's Farm

RH 1 2 3 4 1 2 3 4
LH 5 4 3 2 1 3 2 1

Bb Minor: Baby's Buggy

RH 4 1 2 3 1 2 3 4
LH 2 1 3 2 1 4 3 2

A# Minor: Adoring Aunty

RH 4 1 2 3 1 2 3 4
LH 2 1 3 2 1 4 3 2

Eb Minor: Elephant's Ego

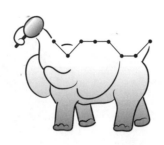

RH 3 1 2 3 4 1 2 3
LH 2 1 4 3 2 1 3 2

D# Minor: Daring Dreamer

RH 3 1 2 3 4 1 2 3
LH 2 1 4 3 2 1 3 2